T0129695

I AM A
MIRACLE

I AM A
DAUGHTER

NKIRU DENKY

WESTBOW
PRESS®
A DIVISION OF THOMAS NELSON
& ZONDERVAN

WestBow Press books may be ordered through booksellers or by contacting:

WestBow Press
A Division of Thomas Nelson & Zondervan
1663 Liberty Drive
Bloomington, IN 47403
www.westbowpress.com
1 (866) 928-1240

ISBN: 978-1-9736-8805-1 (sc)
ISBN: 978-1-9736-8804-4 (e)

Print information available on the last page.

WestBow Press rev. date: 07/31/2020

When it looked like the work of creation was
not complete God made a woman.

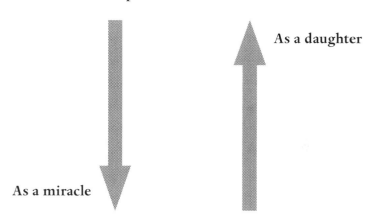

As a daughter

As a miracle

CONTENTS

ACKNOWLEDGMENT

Surely this project couldn't have been if it wasn't first given. I cannot thank God almighty enough, for the privilege given to me to carry out this assignment.

My sincere appreciation goes to Pastor Mrs. Oshode for the time she took off her busy schedule to review this work. Also, the objective feedback of Pastor Mrs. Ebun Aiku was instrumental in the quality of the book. I'm deeply grateful.

To my amazing children, thanks for your understanding, during the brief period of absence trying to bring this dream to fruition

Finally, to my loving, and supportive husband: my deepest gratitude. You were there, from start to finish, giving your vital support.

PREFACE

Look at the cover again and inhale the title of this book because you are going on a journey of discovery regarding the mystery surrounding your existence.

Imagine a tiny day-old human with eyes closed swaddled in a cozy blanket, sleeping peacefully, vulnerable, calm, and ignorant of her surroundings. In between her light but fast breaths, she emits a high-pitched cry when she needs attention because she didn't anticipate it will look so bright, cold, and noisy outside.

Her mother stands nearby in wonder, beholding a little version of herself. She travels back in time, reflecting on her mother staring at her own brilliant small eyes.

Across generations, there has been a continuous procreation obligation reverberating all the way to this era by God's order.

Be fruitful and multiply (Genesis 1:28 NLT)

Childbirth is one of the incredible moments of life and the results so often described as a bundle of joy. Because life is given, which enkindles ceremonies such as naming and child dedications. There is jubilation because life is given and the parents join in acknowledging the mystery.

As days turned into weeks and weeks into years, the child grows into her world, a blossoming flower, developing her wings, her inward abilities, and her unique styles. She sees adventure and possibilities, but her vulnerability runs along with her.

She is perceived as a mother in a girl.

Miracles are the product of wonders, and daughters undeniably confirm that.

INTRODUCTION

Anyone who practices agriculture knows that preparing seedlings and nursery beds before planting is valuable to a farmer. It gives a glimpse of what the end product will be. The farmer fashions the plants. Individual seedlings are given special treatment and as a result, they are kept in bags to protect them from the harsh effect of the environment and pamper them with favorable growth conditions.

Wholesome seeds are a basic necessity for plants to thrive and survive. Seed-bearing plants determine the effect of the germination rates and quality. Seeds are well planned and managed. These are essential steps to achieve optimum results.

In certain circumstances, seeds are labeled for recognition. God saw that it was good.

And I know you by name (Exodus 33:17 NLT).

Seeds are sowed fresh. Then farmers prepare a conducive environment for them to thrive, waters them, and protects them from danger. Once they germinate, the farmer dispatches them carefully to his preferred habitant until maturity and harvesting.

Strolling down the field, the farmer begins scattering the seeds, some fall on thorns and are choked, others are eaten by rat and squirrels eat them up, and few others on fertile ground. These seeds are the survivors like you.

When my bones were being formed, carefully put together in my mother's womb, when I was growing there in secret, you knew that I was there. (Psalm 139:15 GNT)

Seeds are planted in different seasons and for various purposes. And God saw that it was good.

A suitable organ was prepared and you were carefully deposited from His treasure house to your mother's womb in a particular season and time within a generation. He nourishes the newly planted seed, ensures adequate rain and sunlight by planting it in a favourable season. He destroys weeds that tamper with its growth.

When the plants are not flourishing, the farmer sorrows and deploy a solution by applying fertilizer and, if needed, prunes to get them to blossom again.

The farmer carries out these duties diligently with high expectations while waiting in anticipation of a reward for labor.

They produced a crop that was thirty, sixty, and even a hundred times as much as had been planted. (Mathew 13:8 NLT)

From conception to the time you burst forth with that first cry, God almighty has been with you. The Ageless One provides you with everything that pertains to life and godliness.

You were chosen amidst other seeds. You didn't come in other decades and eras, because there is a need for your existence in such as time as this.

By His divine power, He tends and shapes you, but never despise your needs, trials, and life challenges for they are continually before Him. He ensures your adequate satisfaction, while he waits until the day you recognize and call Him Father. Then He can establish a father-daughter relationship with you. In you, He deposited traits to yield good produce, to honour His efforts and become His bountiful harvest.

God wants us to know that we are a distinctive seed in His nursery bed the day we were planted into our mother's womb.

To God, I am His miraculous act and I am His daughter.

I am a miracle to my parents and I am a daughter, a heritage of God. I am under their tutelage. Their home is my first place of contact on earth.

To my husband, I am a miracle and a wife. Before God, my father's name was changed to his, our children bear his name and I am a helpmate perfectly suitable for him.

What are the things that have become the normal we no longer acknowledged?

I found favour when I was chosen among other seeds, the planter performed all rudiments of planting practice and now expects a high yield to commensurate his labor.

The inspiration to write this book came to regenerate, heal, restore and motivate. As you journey through these pages, I pray that the Lord will brood over you to soak in the entire purpose.

I AM A
MIRACLE

SPIRITUALITY

Sunday is the day of the Lord in Christendom.

It has always been a special day, set aside to worship the Most High God.

The core principle of Sunday is for warm-hearted people to gather in a space, lifting their hearts and hands in worship as the choir and band lead the congregation to the throne of grace. As well, the undiluted word of God sets hearts on fire, enriching souls, which is expedient for teaching, direction, counseling, exhortation, rebuking, rectification, and training in righteousness.

You never leave the Master's presence unfulfilled.

As the large gathering of people dressed in their best, but not a beauty contest, the Lord's eye rests on the property, appreciates beauty and delights in its warmth.

NEW LIFE

The crack of the closets indicates they can't handle any more clothes. Humming while flipping through the coloured hangers to fill the closet, I heard chattering and laughter from the next door and noticed on the clock that it's midnight.

I opened the door to find my children's beaming faces with their knees on the floor surrounding a table they were drawing and colouring in a book. I slowly walked into the room, a sharp hiss escaping me as I sat heavily on the black chair. With both hands on my chin, it dawns on me that adapting to Canadian time zone is not happening anytime soon.

It was one month previous that we relocated from my home country to Canada. I worked six hours back and figured out it's 6 am back home and they'd dozed yesterday at 4 pm.

Strolling down the footpath, I observed the beautiful landscape and blossoming flowers in my new neighborhood. The yellow lilies across the green vegetation is breathtaking, but the chill of Canadian spring sends us back to our apartment sooner than we hoped. The new normal was 19C compared to 32C back home.

We were informed by friends to prepare for much worse weather as the temperatures could drop to -45C in our new home of Winnipeg, Manitoba.

Delighted as we were making progress and settling fast, but it wasn't complete as we haven't found a place of worship yet, we resolved to be in church the next Sunday. I grabbed my phone and searched for the nearest Redeemed Christian Church of God. I got my answer, showed it to my husband, we noted and saved the detailed address.

Four months later, my pastor's wife called to confirm the information I gave and enquire about my abilities. I told her I was willing to serve in the choir or the children's department. Because there was an urgent need in the children's ministry, I started the following Sunday.

The choices we make can serve as an indefatigable commitment or feeble decisions which lead to truancy.

I have come to realize that if I'm adequately engaged and serving in an organization, my tendency to leave is minimal. When I'm appreciated for work well done, there is wholeheartedness and desire to contribute even more.

Accepting work in the children's department is one of the reasons I stayed put and shunned the idea of looking for yet another church.

People go to church for many different reasons and purposes. Some prefer belonging to one denomination or the other. Some like the preaching of one pastor over another. Some make friends in a church. It all comes to personal preferences.

In April 2019, after a particular Sunday service, I came to what I call my metamorphosis after an astonishing day in the children department. Ministering to children is a two-way street, but the reward always overshadows the wearisome effect.

Resting at home, just a few minutes we arrived from the service, I heard God speak clearly to me. **"You are going to have a baby, her name, gender, and purpose of birth was given."**

It happened within a matter of seconds and the voice varnished leaving me to ponder on what just happened. My husband and I hadn't planned on having another baby. Our prayer was for God to visit other families trusting God for the fruit of the womb.

Indeed, the Sovereign Lord never does anything until he reveals his plans to his servants. (Amos 3:7 NLT)

POWER OF APPOINTMENT

Now to Him who is able to do immeasurably more than all we ask or imagine according to His power that is at work in us. (Ephesians 3:20 NIV)

According to the old adage, the fruit does not fall far from its tree.

The evolution of technology is to benefit the world as its needs and wants change continuously, like gold in its raw state when refined, it becomes profitable.

God wired each one of us adequately. According to science, the biology of the human body involves cells, tissues, organs, and systems such as cardiovascular, digestive, endocrine, digestive, reproductive system that all function together to make up a living being.

Male mammals typically have an X and Y chromosome (X, Y) while female mammals have two X chromosomes (X, X)

Biologically, the sex of a fetus is determined by five factors at birth:

1. The presence or absence of a Y chromosomes
2. The type of gonads

3. The sex hormones
4. The genitalia (such as the uterus in the females)
5. The external genitalia

A human fetus does not develop its external sexual organs until seven weeks of gestation. At this point, mothers barely know that they are pregnant.

Neither the doctors nor the expectant mother can detect the sex of a naturally conceived baby, except revealed by God.

I knew you before I formed you in your mother's womb. Before you were born I set you apart. (Jeremiah 1:5 NLT).

An interesting factor about a miracle is the instant effect it produces where needed.

My sister-in-law was travelling to the United States to celebrate the college graduation of her niece. My husband was also attending, so we seized the opportunity to have her bring some Nigerian food items from my wonderful mother Lovina Ogbuji.

When my husband arrived home, I welcomed him briefly, then pounced on the fully loaded baggage, unpacking the edibles we'd been eagerly awaiting. Impetuously, I grabbed a dried fish, washed and pieced it up, and gave some to my husband just like Eve gave Adam the forbidden fruit.

Several minutes later, frequent trips to the restroom took over the day. Blinded by my ignorance. I'd forgotten the fish traveled miles and days before it was delivered to us and had turned bad. I was advised to take Imodium for quick relief, which I rejected uttering jokingly: "I could be expecting a child."

Faith is confidence in what we hope for and assurance about things we do not see. (Hebrews 11:1 NIV)

A few weeks later, my doctor confirmed that a miracle has been formed within me and nine months later, our precious princess was born.

"Genuine miracles were not slow, progressive processes; rather, they produced instantaneous effects. Note: [A]nd straightway he received his sight (Mark 10:52 ASV). [A]nd immediately his feet and his ankle bones received strength. (Acts 3:7 ASV).

When Jesus performed signs, even his enemies did not deny the effect of such; they merely attempted to attribute his power to some other source (e.g., Satan; cf. Matthew 12:24 ASV). The leaders of the Jewish community did not doubt that Peter and John had performed a notable miracle when they healed the lame man at the temple; rather, they sought to mute the sign's impact by threats of violence (cf. Acts 4:14ff ASV).

A supernatural display of divine power is not an arguable proposition; it is a dramatic, demonstrable fact. No where in the New Testament is there a record of a divine spokesman arguing for the validity of miracles. No logical scheme is needed to establish such a case. Miracles either happen, or they don't."

-Wayne Jackson, What Does the Bible say about Miracles (Christian Courier).

BECAUSE A DAUGHTER IS BLESSED

Seeds are planted in different seasons and for various purposes. I wouldn't be relevant if I came in the 1930s. But because there is a specific consequential assignment for me to accomplish, I arrived in the 1980s to execute it.

The Lord is good and does what is right. (Psalms 25:8 NLT).

In my father's house, I am his little girl under his watch and guidance. When I mature for marriage, my husband comes for me because I have been equipped to possess the momentous resource fit for a helpmeet.

I am essential in this generation for my children to come through me. I am beneficial to my place of employment by utilizing knowledge gained through education.

As a result, I add value to society. As a daughter of the Most High God, I am a light to the world.

You are the light of the world—like a city on a hilltop that cannot be hidden. (Mathew 5:14 NLT)

All of this is possible because I am in my time. The unfathomable role God gave me to carry and bring forth children through procreation is an honor and a privilege. He specifically gave me the ability to co-create this mystery with and for Him.

There is a special grace released for this incredible nine-month journey. By divine order, multiple spermatozoa were produced, but mine was picked.

Often, pregnant women are vulnerable not because pregnancy is a sickness or disease, but because extra care and caution are needed since new life is involved.

During pregnancy, my water breaking is the rupture of the amniotic sac that indicates my baby is almost ready to be born. No one knows what triggers the chemical chain reaction that begins labor around week 40 of pregnancy.

So many little mysteries are involved.

Who laid out the tremendous belly line (Linea nigra) on baby bumps?

Who formed the umbilical cord and placenta that deliver food to the baby and excrete waste through the expectant mother's body?

Who commands the baby to head downward in preparation to enter the world?

Why do babies cry immediately after birth?

And how do they develop their sucking ability, right after delivery?

How does a mother of twins or triplets produce enough milk to breastfeed all her children?

How is breastmilk uniquely designed to meet the developmental needs of a baby?.

How does breastfeeding create the perfect bond between mother and child?

Why after nine months, does the womb that increased like a ball, shrink back to its pre-pregnancy state.

I watched a documentary about a preterm baby born at 25 weeks. Although the baby's ribs and body skeleton are undeniably visible; it is almost without body fat. I observed the rhythm of the breathing, chest racing up and down, very delicate as if it won't last the next minute, the faltering looks of the mother, the medical equipment placed all over its body. Still, the baby survived and went home 90 days afterward.

Just as you cannot understand the path of the wind or the mystery of a tiny baby growing in its mother's womb. (Ecclesiastes 11:5 NLT).

In the olden days it was reported that women gave birth in their farmland and at home in my home country. But certain modern age mothers are admitted to the hospital at five months or less for close monitoring until their child is born.

On the day the child is dedicated and christened, my pastor often says women have stories to tell about their incredible journeys, in appreciation of what the Lord has done. What about the wonder in women who carry and deliver twins, triplets, and quadruplets?

If you don't know my story, my glory is a mirage.

You are worthy, O Lord, our God, to receive glory and honor and power, for you created all things, and they exist because you created what you pleased. (Revelation 4:11 NLT)

What a mighty God!

THE PRICE

A woman giving birth to a child has pain because her time has come, but when her baby is born, she forgets the anguish because of her joy that a child is been born into the world. (John 16:21 NIV)

In between conception and parturition, there is a battle. From morning sickness, frequent visits to the washroom and constipation to swollen ankles and feet, fear of miscarriage, and midnight aches. Sometimes there are complications like high blood pressure, gestational diabetes, and preterm labour, and some women even lose their lives while giving birth.

After childbirth, an entirely different phase begins. Nursing the baby, keeping immunization records and enduring sleepless nights. At different stages, the baby will begin to smile and laugh, sit, crawl, stand, and walk.

As the child is growing, the choice of food and clothing is reckoned with and closely monitoring against danger. At this period, the baby's life is a clean slate and many forces are in play fighting to shape it. But the most active voice takes preeminence.

To achieve optimum results, if a plant is not growing well, the farmer applies fertilizer and prunes when necessary.

Whether you came through vaginal birth, or C-section (the two basic birth methods), there's an effort, the labour pains, and major surgery soreness, but all dissipate Immediately after the cry of a baby is heard. The world acknowledges a wonder, a mystery through God's work in creation. The price is paid from generation to generation to maintain the chain of procreation.

PHENOMENAL AND REMARKABLE

Life has intriguing phases, from infancy to old age.

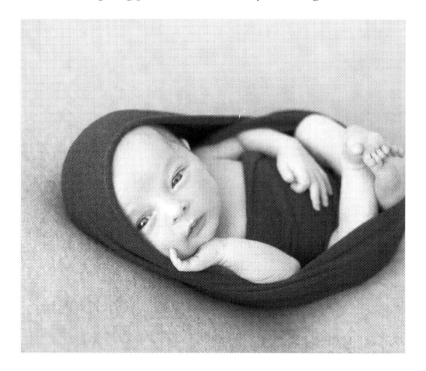

Image is from freepik.com

How beautiful are your sandaled feet
O queenly maiden
Your rounded thighs are like jewels
The work of a skilled craftsman.
Your navel is perfectly formed
Like a goblet filled with mixed wine
Between your thighs lies a mound of wheat
Bordered with lilies.
Your breasts are like two fawns
Twin fawns of a gazelle.
Your neck is as beautiful as an ivory tower
Your eyes are like the sparkling pools in Heshbon
By the gate of Bath-rabbim
Your nose is as the tower of Lebanon
Overlooking Damascus.

Your head is as majestic as Mount Carmel and the sheen of your hair
radiates royalty
The king is held captive by its tresses.
Oh, how beautiful you are?
How pleasing, my love, how full of delights.
(Song of Solomon 7:1-6 NLT)

We are well endowed; each of us emerged distinct from God's imagination.

To thrive, we need to set this daily reminder of what has gone in and prices paid for us to be here.

I am not too dark and not too light.

My breast is in the right proportion.

My body size is made for me.

I am the best version of myself, my fingerprint is strictly mine.

I exist and stand not to be devalued in any circumstance. I came into the world perfectly structured and packaged because God never makes a mistake.

The undeniable truth which will remain until eternity is this: there will always be someone that is prettier, younger, more intelligent, more ingenious, and more prosperous, but they will never be and more human than you. Even more so, they will never be you. There is no comparison between heavenly bodies; each of them emits light and radiates when it's their turn.

Contraception may have failed, news of a missed period may not have been welcomed, here are some truths you need to ponder in your heart.

You are not a biological mishap.

You are not a miscalculation.

You are not an embarrassment.

You are not a deterrent.

You are not a punishment.

You are the seed that was planted when and where it's adequately needed.

I AM A
DAUGHTER

UNABRIDGED EDITION

Across generations, there is a remarkable bond between fathers and their female offspring. Fathers are usually their daughter's first love.

Fathers contribute immensely in molding their daughter's self-esteem and self-worth, and set a positive example for their daughters on how to handle the world. They perform duties that help shape her into a confident and courageous woman as well as proffer solutions on the best methods to express emotions and feelings.

A daughter holds the heart and attention of the father, and she is easily favoured.

SECURED POSITION

May our daughters be like graceful pillars carved to beautify a palace.
(Psalms 144: 12 NLT)

Women may be born as daughters, but they're also destined to live as a princess as well. Princesses have an office, they are the pride of the kingdom, their life radiates from the throne of their father, who is delighted in her. Princesses are obligated to function and execute specific duties in favour of the kingdom. Splendour shines all around her.

The clothes designed for daughters will never suit their male siblings. In families, daughters are seen as a flower, always associated with beauty. Beauty registers in the brain and sends signals through facial expression, and as such, is appreciated.

A female child is always intended to emit beauty into the home. She is under her father's care and he regards her as his little girl even when she is married and in her own home. After all, she was under his leadership before marriage.

In certain tribes in my home country, a daughter is required to kneel on the floor while greeting her father. In many scenarios, fathers even demand to know their destinations.

As the girl grows to a certain age, she prepares and serves her father's meals. She waits until he is done eating and carries the empty plates away. If the meal was delicious, he opens a conversation with appreciation for her that often leads to expositions and profitable success tips. In that state she is open to receive whatever she ask for.

The father sees the female child as one that cares for his well being besides his wife because an everlasting bond is established.

There are limitations to having fathers around the clock because there are friends to visit and errands that demand our attention. And when girls become teenagers and grow into adults, they leave home to pursue their life ambitions.

The Holy Spirit dwelling inside us means we carry God's presence with us everywhere we go. Whenever we mention "in Jesus' name," He is there.

We can serve our heavenly Father the same mouth-watering delicacies as our earthly father. except our service is our worship. After rendering our service, wait until he consumes it. Make it acceptable by building a worthy life suitable to house Him.

A daughter is commissioned unto good works to cement her position. She is seen in ministry: some as pastors, others in the church choir, and various departments such as ushering, children, evangelism, and unto other works of service.

As much as we are relevant in our father's house, our heavenly Father deserves far better.

You will never be outside of He who formed you to be, and that is a daughter. Woman, wear your crown proudly; it is a gift from God that is custom made and will never fit anyone else. Your seat will never be vacant!

Serve wholeheartedly, cement your position, you are the jewel in the crown of God's love.

ADEQUATE PROVISION

The Lord is my shepherd; I have all that I need. (Psalms 23:1 NLT)

My body needs air, water, food, and my soul needs the way, truth, and life.

It isn't about a Rolls Royce but the necessities of life. The 2020 Rolls-Royce Cullinanin is currently valued at $325,000, but the fundamentals of God's Kingdom are free of charge. Let's divide these into two major categories:

1. water, air, and food
2. way, truth, and life.

Looking at the second category, my soul needs the undiluted word of God to grow and thrive as a believer. Salvation through Jesus is free and offers everything I need to learn about life and godliness and how to function in the body of Christ.

There is no gate fee to enter God's holy church. When you say in the name of Jesus, His awesome presence envelopes you.

If the roof over our head is removed, we will become wanderers on the surface of the earth. If He removes sleep from us, our body will collapse.

But He provides the means through the works of our hands and meets our daily needs through trade and by barter: which is the exchange of money to get food that gives us calories and varieties of nutrients, including carbohydrates and protein daily. There is an abundance of air, sunlight, and rain for our lawns, crops, and animals.

Furthermore, He promises to bless our food and water, and true to His word, it nourishes our body.

GUARDIANSHIP

Back home, if there is a trait a girl displays, people will ask who trained her; who is her father? In many cases, after accomplishing a task for a neighbour, they will thank her by saying "your parents are blessed."

One of the responsibilities of fathers is to counsel their children and particularly females. Fathers are coaches, they are ladders, seed bearers, mentors, and a priest in the home.

My child, listen when your father corrects you. Don't neglect your mother's instruction. (Proverbs 1:8 NLT)

Through this training, earthly fathers embedded acceptable characters to mold their female offspring and to also protect their family name.

In my hometown when a girl either by accident or carelessness breaks her pot of water on her way to the stream, she might say "my father will kill me." Not literally, but because of the standard set in that home.

Earthly fathers have a way of influencing the choice of career for their daughters. On many occasions, they verbalize an ideal husband figure to their girls, by using themselves as an example.

They have the ability to discover areas in which their daughters will shine in life endeavours.

Making decisions is part of life, but bad choices can affect our tomorrows. Our future success is significantly impacted by the choices we make today. Decision making is always difficult with many living in regret because of bad choices.

Through the Holy Spirit, God can guide, mentor, coach, and counsel single women in choosing life partners. He can reveal the country to reside, career choice, business ideas, even the number of children to have, and other critical life decisions. He can also inform you when danger looms and way of escape.

When my heavenly Father informed me about what He wanted to do in my life, my countenance changed. Because I knew it was for His own glory and to my advantage. If you have Him steering your life, rest assured that the ship will not sink. He is the Almighty God.

To be part of what God does every season, your spiritual antenna needs to be tuned on at all times. Remove the wax from your spiritual ears.

He can speak to us in many ways: dreams, visions, prayer sessions, studying God's word, and through prophets to name a few.

Anything that doesn't come from Him can expose us and make us defenseless.

The Lord will guide you continually,
giving you water when you are dry

and restoring your strength.
You will be like a well-watered garden,
like an ever-flowing spring.
(Isaiah 58:11 NLT)

Daily chores and cooking management are part of our lives, many times not planned.

You stroll into your washroom to brush your teeth, you notice spilled water on the floor, so you quickly get a mop and bucket and start cleaning. From there, you enter the kitchen and staring at you is a dirty plate on the kitchen counter by the time you're done one hour is gone and you still need to fix breakfast. No matter what, women are caregivers by default.

Caregiver to our husbands, to our parents, to our children, so thankfully our heavenly Father reminds us He will continually restore your strength!

After going through childbirth, you bounced back radiating strength even years later. Bringing another human to the world is not for the faint of heart. Your body expanded and shrinks back, tissues expand and was pressurized.

Your heavenly Father comes with assurance: *You will be a well-watered garden, like an ever-flowing spring.* (Isaiah 58:11)

PROTECTION

The female child sees possibilities, yet her parents see danger and uncertainty. They want her to become a healthy and successful woman, but the world can impose danger. She falls and staggers back as she reaches for the stars.

In her father's house, she is under his protection, but when she marries the responsibility transfers to her husband.

We have undoubtedly accepted that the female child is vulnerable, but how do we protect the female gender against devourers? In today's world, we hear unimaginable acts. Biological fathers molesting and abusing their female offspring, as well as a husband beating and even killing wife in domestic violence.

A king is obligated to protect his kingdom. The life of every girl child is sacred unto God.

If the foundation is destroyed, what can the righteous do? (Psalm 11:3 ESV)

There was a lady who was a beauty queen by all standards and her neighbours thought she lived a perfect life with her husband. In fact, they were building a mansion until tragedy struck. She appears well ornamented, flaunting expensive clothes and jewelry. But her marriage was going through turmoil.

Her smiles and laughter were covering up domestic violence. It destroyed her, but others thought their marriage was heaven on earth.

Are you in an abusive relationship? Speak up and be honest and seek proper counsel so you don't die before your time.

WHO IS MY MOTHER?

My mother is one of the two who created my life. She was right there when life was conceived, and her womb is the medium through which a seed was delivered into the world. She equally wants her children to grow up to become healthy, happy, and prosperous. She is brave and a pillar of support to her children.

Never! Can a mother forget her nursing child? Can she feel no love For the child she has borne? But even if that were possible, I would not forget you! (Isaiah 49:15 NLT)

Mothers and daughters have a lot to share. From beauty tips to career advice or relationship counsel, they are unified in a bond that supersedes blood relations. When a mother and a daughter are buddies, they almost become part of each other. Mothers are often described as more resolute and less reactive, and as a result, have more connection with her.

Because molestation and child abuse are on the rise, girls are most vulnerable, and the relationship between people under the same roof should be closely monitored. The relationship between siblings, cousins, stepbrothers, and stepfathers should be clearly defined. There has been a case of a young girl raped to death by her stepfather, under the same roof with the mother without her knowledge.

Know the state of your flocks and put your heart into caring for your herds. (Proverbs 27:23 NLT)

Protecting younger daughters from sexual harassment and abuse is essential. Teach them the power of their crown as daughters of the most high God, open the door of boldness, and shut the door of intimidation. Give them Jesus early as they need Him.

It's wisdom to educate female offsprings about the wages of sin and the dangers of alcohol, drugs, disobedience, stubbornness, social media influence, pornography, and gambling.

When you follow the desires of your sinful nature, the results are very clear: sexual immorality, impurity, lustful pleasures, idolatry, sorcery, hostility, quarreling, jealousy, outbursts of anger, selfish ambition, dissension, division, envy, drunkenness, wild parties, and other sins like these. Let me tell you again, as I have before, that anyone living that sort of life will not inherit the Kingdom of God. (Galatians 5:19-21 NLT)

Daugther, do you fully respect your parents? Have your parents resigned to their fate because they cannot control you any longer? You need to know that for every action, both good or bad, there is a consequence

When you dig a well, you might fall in. When you demolish an old wall, you could be bitten by a snake. (Ecclesiastes 10:8 NLT).

Our vulnerability runs with us. Mothers (and fathers and brothers) can only protect us to a certain extent. But know this:

I will protect those who trust in my name. (Psalm 91:14 NLT)

Our God knows the ending from the beginning. He sees all the evil plans of men. He sees the attacker and the attacked. He also knows means they planned to execute their acts.

The Lord is watching everywhere, keeping his eye on both the evil and the good. (Proverbs 15:3 NLT)

Position yourself and allow God to guide you, He can't force Himself on you, you need to surrender. Get to a level where He orders every step you take. It is rewarding to be led by the holy spirit of God. A fervent prayer life, inviting the presence of God, and continual pleading for mercy will always save the day.

LIFEMATE

When I sprout up to a full adult, it is natural that suitors will start coming. When my husband appeared, and he meets my requirement, it will be in my interest to get approval from my heavenly Father. Choosing a life partner is not an emotional adventure.

It is the most important decision of your life and if you get it wrong you will live with the outcome for the rest of your life. You simply can't afford to make this crucial decision without Him.

The sure way to identify your life mate when he comes knocking is through prayerful consultation with your heavenly Father. If you try and influence the outcome by rejecting the Father's best advice the opportunity could pass you by. Some ladies are left waiting for Mr. Perfect because they missed a previous opportunity God gave them.

Our God is all-knowing. One of His benevolent acts to His daughters is to reveal what is to come and carelessnessly ignoring His direction can be disastrous. When He shows me the way, I am expected to act accordingly. If His answer is no, don't get carried away with handsome looks and the size of a pocketbook because both can fail.

In my hometown, on the traditional marriage day, a woman kneels and offers her husband a drink in full view of the parents, family, and guests. This connotes recognition and the husband as the head in their union.

A wife being submissive in marriage is not an act of brainwashing or suppression but in love and because it's God's way. When we obey this structure, we create a functional home, and our watchful children will take this down to their generations.

Two are better than one, because they have a good reward for their labor. (Ecclesiastes 4:9 KJV)

COURAGE

Dare fear, Trample on it, peel and crush it into tiny particles.

Grind and process it into powdered form.

Lift it, allow the wind to finish the job, and remember it no more.

Like a baby staggering, mastering her steps as she learns how to walk, take the bold step again and again and again.

"Fear is a response, courage is a preference."

In the book of Esther, we find a woman who displays inordinate courage in the face of a planned genocide of her Jewish people by Haman. Queen Esther's relative Mordecai discovered the evil plan and sent a message informing her. He asked her to go to the king on behalf of the Jews.

Queen Esther was a brave and fearless woman even when it wasn't convenient. She could have died, but she was loyal to her people, and through her, the Jews were saved from destruction. She recognized her abilities and used her position to save a nation.

Queen Esther replied, "If I have found favor with the king, and if it pleases the king to grant my request, I ask that my life and the lives of my people will be spared." (Esther 7:3 NLT)

Deborah is another woman of courage we find in the Bible. The wife of Lappidoth, she was also a prophet who was one of Israel's judges in her time.

Her bravery gave Israel victory over Sisera. Barak realized what God deposited in her and sought her opinion on how to defeat Sisera. Indeed, God honoured her courage and faith in Him.

"Very well", she replied, "I will go with you but, you will receive no honor in this venture for the Lord's victory over Sisera will be at the hands of a woman." So Deborah went with Barak to Kedesh." (Judges 4:9 NLT)

It takes bravery to move from point A to point B in life. It takes unwavering guts to wake up in the morning, dress up, go to work or school, engage in other daily activities, and repeat the same consistently. It involves self-belief to climb the ladder of success and record achievements in the course of our lives, from teen to old age.

Difficulties and challenges will knock at our door from time to time. What do you do when you face these battles?

You need to know this and figure out what to do, for there is going to be trouble for our master and his whole family. He's so ill-tempered that no one can even talk to him!"

Abigail wasted no time. She quickly gathered 200 loaves of bread, two wineskins full of wine, five sheep that had been slaughtered, nearly a bushel of roasted grain, 100 clusters of raisins, and 200 fig cakes. She packed them on donkeys

]and said to her servants, "Go on ahead. I will follow you shortly." But she didn't tell her husband Nabal what she was doing. (1 Samuel 25:17-19 NLT).

What is that situation threatening you? Could it be financial crisis, Drug addiction, health crisis, marital challenges, sicknesses, loneliness, poverty, hardship, afflictions, barrenness...the list is endless.

Look inward, surely there is a battle that has been won for you in the time past, where God that helped you before can help you again. He will surely give you victory over the challenges you face today.

Daughter of God for every obstacle in your path, God will send someone or something for you to defeat it. God is one call away!

It takes courage to give and get involved in other charitable works when you are also struggling financially and emotionally. I don't need to have a lump sum amount of money in my bank account before I can extend helping hands to the needy because I do it unto the Lord.

It takes true contentment with the Lord to remain stable in this generation full of fantasies. If your earthly father cannot afford it at that moment, just wait and destroy those evil thoughts when they first appear.

The face of deception has no regard for you. The serpent in the garden of Eden didn't factor in how beautiful the surrounding was before deceiving Eve. Beware of men in sheep's clothing, presenting what your parents cannot provide for you in any given circumstance.

Good things in life sometimes come in disguise. The fashion of this world is seasonal; items in vogue now will depreciate even a few months later. Whenever Apple or Samsung is about to launch their product, people pre-order months and weeks ahead, but after a few months, they will release yet another with upgraded features. The decision to buy, whether affordable or not, rests on the shoulders of their targeted audience.

THE CHERISHED

I am that much-needed wellspring that finds expression when I was chosen among other seeds.

I arise and shine, I'm aware of my essences

I am endowed with wisdom, I discern, and I have understanding.

I am bold and gifted, my worth is more than pearls, diamonds, and rubies.

I'm beautiful, and I'm alive.

I'm a home builder and keeper

I'm enterprising, productive, and prosperous.

In my earthly father's house, I illuminate his palace.

Isn't it breathtaking to be counted among God's creation? With the beauty of nature? The sun, the moon, the stars, land and sea, the majestic mountains?

During creation, God looked at all the beautiful things He made, including man but still said something is missing, then he made the woman.

When a man decides to settle down in marriage, he looks up to God for permission, and God directs him.

The man who finds a wife finds a treasure and receives favour from the Lord. Proverbs 18:22 NLT).

He takes a step further to seek permission from the earthly father, who gives his blessings and his daughter's hand in marriage.

I wear different hats in the many stages of life. I function as a daughter to my father, as a sister to my siblings, as a mother to my children, and as a wife to my husband. I am not a property to be coveted. I am God's own, wonderfully crafted.

In my childhood when my sisters and I were sick; my father would buy lots of treats. But to my male siblings, he either gave them a little portion or patted their back saying "boy you will be fine." Favouritism played a role, perhaps because we contributed to making his food, which is a way to a man's heart.

Only ask, and I will give you the nations as your inheritance, the whole earth as your possession. (Psalm 2:8 NLT)

I don't need to be the president's daughter to be favoured.

I don't need to be part of the senator's household to be given a job contract.

I don't need congratulations in the corporate world to receive praise.

All I need is to position myself under God's will and accept what's due in each season.

Charm is deceptive, and beauty does not last; but a woman who fears the Lord will be greatly praised. (Proverbs 31:30 NLT).

A 25-year-old woman is free of wrinkles compared with a 70-year-old whose life has takes its toll.

Many years ago, I battled with self-esteem and identity. When I asked Jesus to be the Lord over my life, I discovered that it wasn't about position, looks, status, title, or relationship. Only God determines our worth and defines us.

I am the daughter of the Most High God

I am His and He is mine.

EMPOWERMENT

In the world today, women are pillars in their homes and society. Often we see women as decision-makers and they are allowed to add to the economic circle at home and in their communities.

Through their income, they participate financially in the growth of their families.

It is the parents' responsibility to guide their daughters through education and, by choice, into strategic training.

We have access to opportunities without reservations and limitations, which presents options in our education pursuit, lifestyle, and careers.

.She finds wool and flax and busily spins it. She is like a merchant's ship, bringing her food from afar. She goes to inspect a field and buys it; with her earnings, she plants a vineyard. She is energetic and strong, a hard worker. She makes sure her dealings are profitable; her lamp burns late into the night.

Her hands are busy spinning thread, her fingers twisting fiber. She is clothed with strength and dignity, and she laughs without fear of the future.

(Proverbs 31:13-14, 16-19 and 25 NLT)

Women contribute tremendously in building families, communities, and nations, achieving success, helping humanity, and maximizing God-given potentials. They are found in almost every profession from engineers, pilots, lawyers, and doctors to ministries such as evangelists, and gospel music stars. Each and every woman is intended to showcase God's glory and excellence. Fundamental requirements have been provided to yield maximum results; therefore, we are obliged to give the best to the world.

We can do and achieve amazing things.

In view of all this, make every effort to respond to God's promises. Supplement your faith with a generous provision of moral excellence, and moral excellence with knowledge. (2 Peter 1:5 NLT)

There is no limit to how far one can go in acquiring knowledge. Besides our careers, we can acquire numerous skills and the internet offers an effective learning platform.

LAZINESS IS NOT FOR ME

The lazy person claims, "There's a lion out there! If I go outside, I might be killed!" (Proverbs 22:13 NLT)

Idleness is a disease and it can limit you. There are certain achievements we can attain if only we take laziness away. Many women depend only on the husband for means of survival. There is a heartwarming sensation experienced by a husband and wife when they complement each other sufficiently. The economic system of the world today demands that both parties deploy resources at their disposal in building families and communities.

Some of us started businesses even while at junior college, saving for a specific task helping in the home, thereby making our parents proud. When you're young is the ideal time to prepare, groom, explore, learn, and build in preparation for the chosen path our Heavenly Father has destined for you.

How often do you hear godliness is next to holiness? Laziness can lead to dirtiness and that unkempt environment can hinder prayers and move of God. One of the easiest prayers is God send your angels to watch over me while I sleep. But is the environment befitting for them to stand on guard for you?

You must keep your camp clean of filthy and disgusting things. The LORD is always present in your camp, ready to rescue you and give you victory over your enemies. But if he sees something disgusting in your camp, he may turn around and leave. (Deuteronomy 23:14 CEV)

One morning before I uttered a word, I heard in my spirit, "you make delicious meals, add cleanliness." I was a victim to this ignorance, immediately I went on my knees to plead for mercy and amended my routine to better accommodate cleanliness. When we shun laziness and keep our house and environment clean, there is less risk of air, water, and food contamination, and our heavenly Father is glorified.

We don't graduate from the school of personal hygiene, it's a daily standard. When the hair scarfs and nets are neglected and hair is untreated you can appear unkempt. Your outer appearance doesn't need to be perfect, but even moderately good can work.

A pleasant smell oozing out of a natural body is a delight you offer to yourself and those around you. Looking good can help you to pass, so invest in your life and shine.

There is a melody that flows from being well-groomed. It feeds confidence and people's perceptions about you. Tighten all corners and firmly reject laziness in regards to your appearance.

FULFILL YOUR DIVINE PURPOSE

And then I discovered my inner light, my exceptional characteristics I took my power back and the music changed.

As expensive as a drum is, if no one is playing that instrument, it's useless and its purpose is hindered and unutilized.

There is something in you that the world needs.

Your gift is an inherent capacity to fulfill a function that meets a need in creation. Inherent means no one can give it to you, you were born with it. Your value is your level of usefulness.

There is a norm about success stories and achievements that delight the soul.

My beloved husband always says that "failure is an orphan while success has children and grandchildren."

People are looking for what you are carrying – not necessarily you – and when they see this manifestation, they rejoice with you.

Everything you need is planted within you. The heavenly Father's desire is for you to prosper, flourish, and be diligent with all the wonderful gifts he entrusted in your care and importantly to use it for His glory. Never underestimate the gift that the Lord has given you.

You must discover and proceed to possess.

Father God is the source of all your gifts and He is inexhaustible.

After a long time, their master returned from his trip and called them to give an account of how they had used his money. The servant to whom he had entrusted the five bags of silver came forward with five more and said, "Master, you gave me five bags of silver to invest, and I have earned five more. The master was full of praise. "well done, my good and faithful servant. You have been faithful in handling this small amount, so now I will give you many more. Let's celebrate together!" (Matthew 25:19-21 NLT)

Talent was utilized and success was achieved.

"The master said, 'Well done, my good and faithful servant. You have been faithful in handling this small amount, so now I will give you many more responsibilities." (Matthew 25:23 NLT)

This means that success begets more success!

Then the servant with the one bag of silver came and said, 'Master, I knew you were a harsh man, harvesting crops you didn't plant and gathering crops you didn't cultivate. I was afraid I would lose your money, so I hid it in the earth. Look, here is your money back.' But the master replied, 'you wicked and lazy servant! If you knew I harvested crops, I didn't plant and gathered crops I didn't cultivate, Why didn't you deposit my money in the bank? At least I could have gotten some interest in it.' Then he ordered, 'Take the money from this servant and give it to the one with the ten bags of silver." To those who use well *what they are given, even more, will be given, and they will have in abundance. But from those who do nothing, even what little they have will be taken away.*

(Matthew 25:21, 24-29 NLT)

As long as you are alive, you have something someone needs.

In the same way, let your light shine before others, that they may see your good deeds and glorify your Father in heaven. (Mathew 5:16 NIV)

You may see yourself running round in circles in confusion. Maybe you have not discovered your gift yet or not using it to the fullest, but the answer is simple: go to your Father in prayer and He will reveal it to you.

There is a space for you at the top. Take hold of your talent and put your best into it. It's never too late. Start now.

Write the vision and make it plain. (Habukkuk 2:2 NKJ)

Stay true to bringing your dreams and aspirations to fruition with diligence, perseverance, and prayer.

Watch your circle, beware of negativity, and draining energy. A viable cycle should include visionaries and go-getters that won't allow you to be passive about fulfilling your purpose.

Eagles and parrots are birds, but something differentiates the two birds; the latter is wordy and can't fly, but the former is wordless but can touch the sky.

Find your purpose, pursue it relentlessly. Your gift is part of your value; fulfill your God-given destiny!

THE CRUCIAL JOURNEY

We are not immune to the challenges of life.

When life throws you a brick, use it as a bridge to cross to the other side! Move forward.

When you go through deep waters, I will be there be with you; when you go through rivers of difficulty, you will not drown. (Isaiah 43:2 NLT)

Often in the rigorous journey of life, when we face trials, temptations, and tribulations, the above passage is the remedy. We are advised by the Holy Spirit to look unto Jesus for answers and guidance.

Our heavenly Father gives us this assurance.

I have told you all this so that you may have peace in me. Here on earth, you will have many trials and sorrows. But take heart, because I have overcome the world. (John 16:33 NLT)

Looking to any other method leads to frustrations, failure and disappointments. Jesus is the perfect answer and solution to every problem.

Dealing with your emotions is a sensitive issue throughout the years. Regardless of your stand, train yourselves to be in control of your responsiveness or else you can lose it.

Emotions are strong feelings deriving from one's circumstances, mood, or relationships with others. Feelings are learned behaviors that are usually in hibernation until triggered by an external event.

Many once happy homes and marriages have shattered, many families are in conflict due to the inability to control anger. Rage can break many a meaningful relationship, cause some to while away in prison and even cut lives short. There are increasing incidents of wives murdering their husbands and killing house helpers and stepchildren. These are undeniably linked to the inability to control temperament.

A person without self-control is like a city with broken-down walls. (Proverbs 25:28 NLT)

Self-control is a fruit of the Holy Spirit. You must have Him first before you can exhibit His traits!

But the Holy Spirit produces this kind of fruit in our lives: love, joy, peace, patience, kindness, goodness, faithfulness, gentleness, and self-control. (Galatians 5:22-23 NLT)

A force is applied to an object to move from its state of rest or to stop moving. The flesh and the Spirit tussle constantly, but the most dominant wins. It is imperative to actively participate by making a firm decision to tune down our natural tendencies towards anger and control or live with lifetime regrets.

People ruin their lives by their own foolishness and then are angry at the Lord. (Proverbs 19:3 NLT).

Our emotions fluctuate and our own understanding is not good enough, in fact, it's limited. But we have the maker of heaven and earth as our Father. Trust Him. That is not an understatement.

Trust in the LORD with all your heart and lean not on your own understanding; in all your ways submit to him, and he will make your paths straight (Proverbs 3:5-6)

When things are not working as planned, I need only turn to my heavenly Father. If it's not as desired or God's plan for my life, I can get stuck and not make progress, but if its the perfect place for me, I will be covered by His abundant grace.

HEALING TO THE BODY AND SOUL

My good health is my fortune. Everything is paramount until sickness comes knocking and then you realize the most important thing is our health. Often we neglect the well we draw water from and instead choose stress, restlessness, and focus on unimportant things. Sickness can hinder the smooth running of life affairs. You can't pour from an empty cup. Always take proper care of yourself.

The terrible past? The pain? The setbacks? The mistakes, scares, failures, and wounds? The rejections and betrayals?

Cut off all ties to these and turn to Jesus, the One who redeems all. His mercy is far more significant and everlasting. When you have received the mercies of God over a confessed sin, personal unforgiveness is a setback.

Mistakes are painful when they occur, but a heart that has been purged by the Master can view them as experiences not to repeat.

People may see a woman with a past, but our God knows us from the very beginning and He sees a woman with purpose and potential. Never permit anyone to discredit your repented status. You may not be able to influence situations, but only you can control your attitude. Advocate against mistakes of the past it means you grew up, and you can actually help the younger generation against such pitfalls.

There is a balm of Gilead, He's Jesus. Only He is the healing balm you need today. He can mend every broken heart, heal every wound and fill every space.

I even I am he who blots out your transgression for my own sake and remembers your sins no more. (Isaiah 43:25 NIV)

It is time to redress and never be afraid to start over, it is a chance to rebuild and rebrand your life the way you wanted it. A long time ago, there was a little girl full of life and ambition, and you can make her proud.

Blessed is she who has believed that the Lord would fulfill his promises to her! (Luke 1:45 NIV)

With God, you are comforted and blessed.

The thief comes only to steal and kill and destroy; I have come that they may have life and have it to the full. (John 10:10 NIV)

The stripes Jesus took on my behalf about two thousand years ago paid for sickness in my body. His blood cleanses me from all my sins. God didn't give me the strength to get back on my feet so that I can run back to the thing that knocked me down. By His ultimate sacrifices, I am healed, restored and completely whole.

Therefore, come out from among unbelievers, and separate yourselves from them, says the lord. Don't touch their filthy things, and I will welcome you. And I will be your Father, and you will be my sons and daughters, says the Lord Almighty. (2 Corinthians 6:17-18 NLT)

He has given us an open and constant invitation and the requirement.

Let both grow together until the harvest. Then I will tell the harvesters to sort out the weeds, tie them into bundles, and burn them, and to put the wheat in the barn. (Matthew 13:30 NLT)

After all the busy bustling of this world, the day of harvest is coming. When a saved soul dies and leaves this world, their Jesus has come.

We are accountable for how we train and nurture the miracles under our care. As a parent sending my children to church and then to turn around and indulge in self-righteousness can't save me. All charitable works don't save. Beauty doesn't save. Salvation can only be attained by confessing my sins, repenting and accepting Jesus Christ in as my Lord and Saviour.

ABBA
FATHER

THE REASON

Couples decide on the number of children to have, places to live, values that will guide their home before they set out on their marriage union, but let's look at some of the reasons why they have children.

Couples decide to have children because everybody does it and it's the social standard. We naturally conform to the pattern when we were born.

Another reason is to keep the family name and lineage across generations.

Many desire a sense of belonging and responsibility as a result of the powerful bond between parents and their children.

God created us in His own image, He blessed us and said be fruitful and multiply and replenish the earth. He created us to bring Him glory and honor.

Our Heavenly Father expects us to bear fruit into his kingdom and influence the world. We influence people, products but most importantly He wants us to influence others about the kingdom of God. We were created unto good works, irrespective of the profession in which you are serving.

The people whom I formed for myself that they might declare my praise. (Isaiah 43:21 ESV)

THE EXPRESSION

We are all expressions of God's distinction.

There are different kinds of spiritual gifts, but the same Spirit is the source of them all. (1 Corinthians 12:4 NLT)

To one of His daughters, He gave the capacity to perform miracles in His name. To the other daughter, He gave the ability to sing and bless lives with her voice. To another daughter, He gave the gift of healing the sick. To others, He gave them the grace to prophesy. There are others who can manifest more than one gift all is to His glory.

The singing bird in the sky and the bubbling sound of the sea leaves on the tree, aquatic animals under the sea. Crawling animals on the surface of the earth and every creature in its habitat. The sun to rule the day and moon to rule the night. The land to be cultivated and bring forth crops. We have always witnessed the day unfolding as the morning, advancing into the afternoon and ending at night in that order across generations. He created all for His glory.

HIS POWER AND GLORY

Beyond human understanding, there is an amazing thing about lightning, rumbling of the thunder, and watching a storm from a distance. It calls to mind an incomparable power and sovereignty of God over all creation.

"To whom you will compare me? Who is my equal?" asks the Holy one. (Isaiah 40:25)

God is enough in power, authority, wealth, wisdom, knowledge, majesty, splendor, honor, and much much more. He is bigger than time, He controls seasons and He doesn't need anything to be God.

He makes people who don't believe in themselves and those that people don't believe in, He makes them great. Out of His belly are the presidents, rulers of nations, governors, pastors, ministers, timbres, and calibers. None of this is farfetched as He is the Master of the universe.

And it is even more amazing and exciting that a powerful king as God is mindful of me. He calls me daughter!

And He does that for you too.

For this reason, you are encouraged to run with Him as you journey through life, looking unto Jesus, the author, and finisher of your faith. Man made resources can fail you, trusted friends can also betray you, but God's promises stand sure until eternity.

Because you are the daughter of the Most High God, you are no longer a slave to sin, to fear, mockery, mediocrity, failure, underachieving, poverty, self-pity and shame. You are invited into an extraordinary father-daughter relationship.

So, you have not received a spirit that makes you fearful slaves. Instead, you received God's Spirit when he adopted you as his own children. Now, we call him, Abba Father (Romans 8:15 NLT)

The outstanding relationship you have with your earthly father can be tied to your heavenly Father. He even prefers to be addressed as a father.

This, then, is how you should pray: ' Our Father in heaven, hallowed be your name, (Matthew 6:9 NIV)

Give Him complete access to step into all the affairs of your life. Give Him your all, He wants it all.

Then the earth quaked and trembled. The foundations of the mountains shook; they quaked because of his anger. Smoke poured from His nostrils; fierce flames leaped from his mouth. Glowing coals blazed forth from him. (Psalm 18:7-8 NLT)

God is a loving Father, but also an all-consuming fire. He is not to be joked with, but feared and revered.

He shot his arrows and scattered his enemies; great bolts of lightning flashed, and they were confused. (Psalms 18:14 NLT)

A mere mortal cannot risk being called an enemy of God, and the only way through Him; to maintain an everlasting relationship is through our Lord Jesus Christ.

But to all who did receive him, who believed in his name, he gave the right to become children of God. (John 1:12 ESV)

Printed in the United States
By Bookmasters